Turnir

Pub

A collection of poems by Shirley Anne Cook

Copyright Shirley Anne Cook 2015

Dedication:
For my mother and father.

Shirley Anne Cook is a poet and an author of books for children and teenagers, published under the name Shirley Harber.

She is a primary school teacher and lived in Egypt for a while, where she taught English. She now resides in Buckinghamshire.

www.shirleyannecook.wordpress.com

Competition Placements

'Sandstorm' won first prize in the Mary Charman Smith poetry competition (2015).

'Who Needs Diamonds Anyway?', 'Nature Walk' and 'The Ant' won the Swanwick Writers' poetry competition (2008, 2011, 2014).

'Feeding a Pharaoh' won the Winchester Writers' poetry competition (2011).

'Man in the Moon' won the *Writing Magazine* poetry competition (2008).

'The Race' won The Artillery of Words poetry competition (2009).

'Summer in the Park' was placed second in The Artillery of Words competition (2010).

'The Tramp' won second prize in the John Clare poetry competition (2010).

'The Quail's Egg' was shortlisted in the Basil Bunting poetry competition (2012) and was runner-up in the *Mslexia* poetry competition (2013).

'Raleigh's Wife' was shortlisted in the *Mslexia* competition (2012).

'The Snowball' was shortlisted in The Chapel Gallery poetry competition (2011).

'Lessons on Lorca' and 'My Father-in-law' were shortlisted in the Plough Poetry Competition (2008).

'Care homes for poets', 'Turning the Map Over', 'Hard to Swallow', 'Soundtrack' and 'Landscapes' were runners-up in the *Writer's Forum* competition (2007 to 2015).

'Ship of Dreams' and 'Watching the Whirling Dervishes' were shortlisted in *Writing Magazine* (2007).

'Eight' was shortlisted in the Mary Charman poetry competition (2014).

'Ancient Gardeners' was shortlisted in *Writing Magazine* (2015).

'Heirloom' was shortlisted in Rhyme and Reason poetry competition (2013).
'Battle of the birds' and 'Verdun' were highly commended in Swansea Writers (2014).

Acknowledgements

Riptide (2013, Dirt Pie Press)
First Time (2012, First Time Publications)
When the Tramp Met the King (2013, Ek Zuban)
Slant of Light (2013, Paragram)
Extinction and Fragile Earth (2012, Baskalier)
Mulled Words: A Winter Anthology (2010, Artillery of Words)
One Word Anthology (2013, Talkback Writers)
Unforgotten. The Great War 1914–1918 (2014, Accent Press)
Rhyme and Reason Diary (2014, Rennie Grove Hospice Care)
Winchester Writers' Conference: The Best of 2011
Writers' Forum
Writing Magazine

Turning the Map Over

By

Shirley Anne Cook

Contents

Turning the Map Over

So I take the Piccadilly line through
dew-laden fields,
everywhere early morning
bird call, no garbled guard call.
A solitary rabbit sits on the platform,
rumbles a warning then scurries
down the subway.

Following a buttercup path I head
to the next stop, the woodland copse.
I breathe in bluebell and wet earth smells –
no nine to five body smells.
Bracken brushes my legs,
a bramble wants to walk with me.
I wander aimlessly. I've no sense
of direction and I'm lost
in all my senses.

I come to the lake.
No-one is breathing
down my neck,
treading on my feet.
I take a seat.
A king-fisher hovers over the water,
a drake says good morning (that's a first)
A swan unfolds its newspaper,
but there's not a trace of print in sight.

The sun is climbing through the trees,
it drenches me in light.
I'm glad I caught
this morning's kingdom
and not the eight-thirty to Earl's Court.

I walk to the end of the line,
and thank God I turned the map over.

The Ant

I find an ant crawling on my hand.
I blow it gently to the floor
and watch it march over the vast
continent of my rug,
its infinitesimal legs
working in sequential manner.
It stops to lift a crumb
bigger than itself to take
back to its nest,
for its queen and colony.
I marvel at the diligence
of this slender-waisted fellow.

It has reached the door.
My husband enters.
But he is not Solomon.
In one second the ant's life is stamped out.
A sadness descends over me.
Will its comrades send a search party?
Will they grieve for this worker,
unsung hero of the insect world?
It is now a pinpoint cipher on the sole of a shoe.
Something of its life should stay.
I have this poem.

Elementary

I am sitting at my dressing table.
The sun streams through the window
and sets my silver jewellery box alight.
An explosion of rainbow colour
dances on the wall in front of me.

I remember physics lessons,
drawing diagrams of prisms,
trying to figure out the direction
the light rays travelled,
discussion about refraction,
dispersion, deviation,
atoms, neutrons and photons.

The spectral colours glow.
Their warmth seeps through
the bones of my feet and rises up and up,
until my whole body pulsates with rainbow
and light leaks from the top of my head.
At this moment nothing else matters,
but that I am here watching the sun
unveil its fingerprints.

First Day of Spring

My mother flings windows open,
'to let the devil out'. She fastens
her Paisley-patterned apron,
gathers weapons of dirt destruction:
scrubbing brush, Ajax, bucket, mop.

I have to polish, but I like the way
the 'Brasso' uncovers lost treasure.
My fingers are liquorice sticks,
as mother, streaming with sweat,
inspects a gleaming plate.
'You're doing a grand job.'
She rolls up Dandycord mats
and takes them outside to wash.
A glint of sunlight – our prints
already collecting dust.

Nature Walk

Back to school.
The smell of new pencils
and black rubber-soled plimsolls.
Mrs Matts pins a poster on the wall.
'What to Look for in Autumn.'
A short talk, then we're off to the woods.
Lee doesn't want to wear his coat.
Mrs Matts says he must.
'There's a nip in the air now.'

We march across the field,
two by two.
The air smells of bonfires and wasped fruit.
Lee and I play football with
a rotting crab apple.

In the woods the sunlight filters through
the trees and bathes
everything in a copper sheen.
Acorns pop beneath my feet
and fallen leaves crackle like cornflakes.
Mrs Matts holds an acorn aloft.
'Giant oak trees grow
from tiny seeds like this,' she says.
Thirty pairs of eyes look up.
I gasp, I can't see the top.
I put acorns in my pocket.

Billy Jones lets out a cry —
he has found a conker tree.
Everyone scrambles on the ground
prizing open thorny pouches,
while squirrels chatter angrily

above our heads.
We walk back to school
then write about Autumn
in new exercise books.

At playtime Billy Jones brags
that his conker is a 'tenner'.
I finger the acorns in my pocket
and dream of giant bean stalks.

Eight

I tell myself it doesn't matter:
the slammed door,
your hasty footsteps on the path,
the missing wave and smile
when I, aged eight,
pressed nose on glass,
hopeful of your return.

I tell myself it doesn't matter
how I waited there until late
refusing food and ignoring
Father's demands to go
to bed, where each night
I cried myself to sleep.

I tell myself it doesn't matter
that I started to hate you;
you who gave me life
and loved me for eight years.

I tell myself it doesn't matter
that you never sent a letter
or remembered special days.

And it doesn't matter that
I never saw you again.
I've been just fine without you.
So you see, it doesn't matter.

Christmas Presents

Each Christmas my father
placed presents beneath
twinkling fairy lights,
wrapped in his bumbling way.
'No peeping,' he'd say.
And then pretend not to see
me tiptoe to the tree.
I miss the games we played.

Summer in the Park

In July 1985 I said goodbye
to primary school days.
I threw my bag high in the air
and shouted, 'School's out forever!'
On the way home me and my mate Jack
stopped at the ice-cream van
and bought huge 99s to celebrate.

We spent that hot summer holiday
in the park, playing football and cricket,
climbing trees and making dens.
We often stayed 'til it grew dark,
hanging out with friends.

Sometimes we caused mayhem
in the little kids' park.
We charged through the sandpit
and sent castles tumbling,
wrapped swings around
the bars so seats were too high to reach,
then whirled on the roundabout
until drunk on spin.

As the holiday drew to a close
we would sit and talk
about our new schools,
wondering what the teachers
would be like and what would happen
if we broke new rules.
Jack was going to the grammar school
on the other side of town,
but he said he'd still be my friend.
Why did that summer have to end?

The Snowball

She holds the snowball
in mittened hands,
satisfied she has patted
a perfect globe.
She presses it to her lips
and gently takes a bite.
Her tongue tingles with the taste
of a thousand dendrites.

Bending down she pushes
the ball across the virgin snow
relishing the crunching sound it makes
as it grows and grows.
Face glowing with exertion
she tramples a twisted
path searching for only the purest snow.

She rests now, enshrouded
in her panting breath,
bones rattling with cold.
She gazes at the snowball
through frosted tears.
It has grown too big to hold.

Hard to Swallow

A willow-whittled snake
my father made,
the long gnarled rod
laid by his knife
at the head of the table.
'No one gets down until
plates are clean.'
His voice was a barbed Bible.

I can still taste the dry liver pieces
that stuck in my throat,
Tuesday's tinned peaches,
like goldfish, served
in thick-skinned custard
and the blood-juiced beetroot
that made me choke.

'Children in Africa would
be thankful for that!'
My father's rage rapped
the back of my hand.
And how I wished and wished
the stick was a wand
to wave it and magic him
gone.

The Tramp

I remember seeing you on my way to school,
shuffling along the road in the shadows,
rummaging in bins or picking over
the smoky ends that had smouldered
in another's lips.
A huddled heap in scarecrow clothes,
you were like a mislaid parcel
tied tightly round
with string.

I remember seeing you in the park
spark out beneath last week's news,
watching the world pass by
with dulled old eyes,
the dregs of broken dreams eddying
at your feet.

I remember seeing you on Christmas Eve,
you smiled and gave a mock salute,
your Father Christmas whiskers
bristling with frosted breath.
My mother's gloved grip
hurried me past, as she muttered
that you'd catch
your death.

And I remember that day
they found your iced bones
on the memorial steps,
ribboned medals lay at your side
and faded poppies wreathed
your head.

Who Needs Diamonds Anyway?

'They're not diamonds, silly,'
Kathy Smith said, pig-tailed, porcelain-skinned,
so pretty she made me sick.
She snatched the brooch from my hand
and ran across the play-ground.
'Miss, she's got my brooch!'
I said to the dinner lady.
'Shouldn't bring jewellery to school.'
'But Miss!'
'Didn't you hear the bell? In now.'

I never saw my brooch again.

There was a school reunion last week,
Kathy Smith was there,
grey-haired, grey-skinned.
'Hello, remember me?'
She gave a giant crow-footed smile.
'Of course I do,' I replied, seething inside.
And while we drank tea she told me how
her husband had walked out and that
she had two sons, both born dead.
'And you?' she asked, nibbling a cream bun.
'Married, five children, three grandsons.'
Not seething so much now.
'I'm sorry I took your brooch,' she said.
'I still have it. Do you want it back?'
'No, they weren't diamonds anyway.'
I got up and walked away.

Lessons on Lorca

It was Easter time,
we ate hot cross buns
filled with butter and jam,
then drank your home-made sangria.
You read my essay on Lorca
and said it needed more
reference to 'duende'.
We listened to Concierto de Aranjuez.
You explained the off-tonic guitar trill,
how it creates the seeds of tension,
mirroring each note with
fast-fingered vibration.

It grew dark.
I got up to go and spilt sangria
on your white sheepskin rug.
You laughed, said I was drunk.
The moon's icy face danced
patterns on the hearth
and I wept silent tears,
as Lorca's 'horseman' came galloping
past and you breathed
'Olé!'

Purple Bike

I was thirteen when Cupid landed
on my door mat – a pink padded satin heart
with a scribbled note.
'Meet me at four by the bridge.'
A two-mile journey for me, ten for him.
My purple bike was a winged chariot.

He was sitting astride his Honda 175
dressed in skinny jeans and leather jacket,
long hair poking out from beneath
his 'Centurion' crash helmet.
We shared an awkward kiss,
it tasted of cider and spearmint.
He laughed because I closed my eyes.
(I'd read in 'Jackie' that's what you did.)
He held my hand and called me cute,
whispered he wanted more.
I made an excuse and sped away,
my tyres hissing home to safety
and Mum's jam sponge for tea.

Soundtrack

Elvis didn't die in August seventy-seven.
He came to live at our house.
He slept with Mum and ate
beans on toast for tea.
During the week he worked
for the gas board, but at weekends
he slicked back his hair
put on his gold lamé suit
and rock and rolled down the pub.

Mum didn't seem to mind
living with Elvis.
She said she liked
the smell of Brylcreem
and the way he curled
his lip and shook his hips.

When we had guests
he'd play his guitar
and sing 'Love me Tender'
or 'Heartbreak Hotel'
and answer questions
with 'uhh huhh' instead of 'yes'.
We'd sip tea in Elvis cups
and eat cake on Elvis plates
and when everyone went home
he'd say, 'Well, thank you very much.'

It took years to erase
my childhood soundtrack,
but now Elvis has left the building
I find myself playing it back.

Raleigh's Wife

My love, I carry you everywhere with me.
This leather bag is like a second womb
and bulges with your head.
It weighs the same as our son at birth,
but you are stillborn.

There are black-cowled whispers.
'Widow Raleigh is insane,' they say.
'Why not a lock of his hair?'
I am undeterred, your embalmed head
will accompany me everywhere.

I like to slip my fingers inside
your crackled cocoon and explore
the geographies of your exquisite face.
My finger tips linger on the curve of rictus lips.
It's as though your laugh has just left.

At night I take you out and bathe
you in sweet-scented herbs,
wreathe you in your finest ruff,
each lace purl pressed to perfection.
Then when it's time to sleep
your head rests on the pillow next to mine.

Your torso may reek of rottenness
but worms will not steal our goodnight kiss.

Thumbing It

My right thumb is twice
the size of the left one.
Such bliss, legs in knee socks,
forefinger crooked over my nose.
It was sweeter than a lollipop.

My mother tried to entice
the tooth twister from its den
with gifts and sharp mustard tang,
but me and my thumb
would not be parted.

'Goofy!' Cries at school finally prised it out.
Far too late, the damage was done:
a braced smile and an ugly thumb.

So I whorled it in gold,
red-varnished the misshapen nail
then set off 'thumbing it' around
the world.

And it came to rest
on a marriage deed –
two peacock eyes nestling
side by side.
'I love every part of you,' he said.
Such bliss, feeling the tip of his tongue
tracing the curve of my thumb.

A Magic Carpet Ride

So we parked our magic carpet,
and found a café in the shade.
We drank sweet tea thick as mud
and watched lizards laze
in clinging vine tendrils.
Around us ancient arched stones echoed
with muezzin's calls to prayer.

You read my fortune in the cup,
said I'd marry a girl with eyes
like the sunlit Bosphorus
and lips the colour of flags strewn above.
We laughed, our faces touched.

Your eyes have now lost their sparkle.
The flags were taken down
long ago and the magic carpet
is in the attic gathering dust.

Skinny Dipping at Lady Falls

One mile into the wood
we find the moon-bathed pool.
I place the blanket on the ground
and start to undress, you hesitate.
'Maybe this is not such a good idea.'
But it's on my bucket list to do.
I leave my clothes in a neat pile
and slip into the silky blackness.

The ice-cold depths steal my breath,
but soon I'm high on the sensation
of swimming with unfettered skin.
I beckon you in but you want none of this,
so with a flash of my new silver-scaled tail,
I swim away, leaving you floundering.

Ship of Dreams

I'm drifting around down here,
here in these dark sea-weeded depths.
I'm a quivering wreck and yes,
I've become adept at reeling
off the odd sea joke.
The fish give me gulped mouth ovations.
I'm their white-boned castle.

It's not easy making friends.
I only have one.
Day and night he skulks around
the bladder-wrack bed
waving his violin bow, saying.
'I never stopped playing
while the ship went down.'
He bores me stiff with his white-pegged
clackety-clack monotone.

I spend my days dreaming back,
back to when I had flesh on my bones,
a soft shimmering skin
and long silken black hair.
I reeked of perfume, not fish,
and dazzling diamonds danced
around my neck.
It's not their sparkle I miss,
but that of the stars.

Ancient Gardeners

Sirius glitters in the night sky
and heralds Akhet,
the season of the Nile flood.
Soon the banks will overflow
with rich black silt – Egypt's life blood.
When the waters recede
farmers will plough the ground,
while women and children
scatter seed around.
This season of sowing they call Peret.
Shemu, harvest time, comes next.
Bronze backs will glisten
and sickles flash in sun god Ra's harsh rays.
When the granaries are full
everyone will sing Amun's praise.

On the tomb walls of Set Maat
artists record this seasonal story.
The ancient gardener's world,
there for eternity.

Landscapes

Every morning she climbs mudbrick steps
to the roof where she hangs washing,
then gazes out over fields of sweet corn.
She watches men in galabayas ride donkeys
along ancient date tree paths,
and ambling black-robed
women sharing cowled tête-à-têtes.
Minarets are skeletal fingers
pointing upwards in the cerulean void.

Once this landscape enthralled her,
but now the sun's white eye saps her strength.
She hates the street stench, the wild dog cries,
the continual intrusion of sand
and crackling of microphone adhans.
She craves the sight of lush English hills,
church steeples, cumulus clouds
and the smell of rain-soaked earth.

Strange how in the throes of love's first embrace
you say, 'I'd live anywhere with you.'
And how soon it becomes not enough.

My Father-in-Law

Every morning at sunrise he rose.
I'd hear him purify his body head to toe:
the spluttering cough, clearing of the nose,
each part cleansed, three times, three times, three times.
Then when washing was complete
he shuffled past my door in sandalled feet
urged by muezzin cries, to the mosque to pray.
He'd repeat that four more times that day.
'Cleanliness is half of faith,' Prophet Mohammed said.

A Family Business

That time in Cairo,
crumbling in the heat,
we went in search of water
and got lost. We wandered narrow
pot-holed back streets
where family life revolves
around rotting refuse heaps.

Black-gowned mothers
clawed at the mounds,
sorting plastic, glass and card.
Fathers and bare-footed children
piled the spoils onto donkey carts.
Goats grazed in the leftover scum,
while a haze of flies thrummed
the putrid air and cockroaches
scurried in the shadows.

A small boy suddenly cried out
and waved a silver spoon.
He ran to show us, eyes glittering
like the sunlit Nile.
You'd think he had found the moon.

Sandstorm

Khamseen-driven sand swirls
and eddies on the balcony.
Every day I sweep and clean.
House-proud. It is the enemy.
The fine red dust seeps into drawers
and mattresses, piles deep in corners,
stains the filigree nets.
It penetrates the darkest orifices.
Rivulets of sweat run down my face.
But I will not be beaten.

Soon I must wash my matted hair,
rinse the gritty grains from my mouth
and tend my scoured skin.
Then the 'dutiful wife' will serve
hot sweet tea in glass cups,
replenish gurgling water pipes,
become 'Scheherazade' again.

But I have planned my escape.
Friday at prayer time
I'll take a taxi by the date grove –
they always wait there.
Then shaking the sand from my clothes
I will quietly leave,
unseen.

Feeding a Pharaoh

There are some jobs you are born to,
I'm well-endowed you see.
'Hung like a cow,' my old man says.
After the birth of our son
my blue-veined globes overflowed
with milkiness.
There was too much for one,
so I found work at the palace.

Now here I sit with a prince's mouth
clamped to my bulbous breast.
And by Horus he has a fierce suck!
He sends my womb into contractions,
my ducts stream with delicious sweetness.
I'm like the River Nile in the season of Akhet,
my he-milk as potent as its rich black silt.

He stops feeding now and sleeps,
a trace of a frown on his baby brow,
and he dreams.
He dreams of the battles he will fight,
the temples he will build and the stone stelae
on which he will record his victories.
And he dreams of a tomb furnished with gold,
its walls inscribed with his life's story.
And I a farmer's wife,
who has nourished a god,
will be a hieroglyph there
for eternity.

Paper Boats on the Nile

We made paper boats that day
and watched as they floated far from our reach
upon the deep blue depths of the Nile,
in suffocating heat.

Through minaretted mayhem we walked,
a 'welcome' smile in man's harsh blare
and muezzin choirs echoed out
sanctifying putrid air.

The 'Mother of the World' beguiled us,
as we trod ancient sweat-marked paths
marvelling at her dripping jewels,
gifts of dynasties long past.

We sat with leather-skinned men
sipped mint tea and puffed on water pipes,
their sweet scents drifted away
embalming the frenzied night.

I wonder where our boats are now.
Did they journey to some forgotten land?
Perhaps one day they'll return,
helms guided by our entwined hands.

My Sister-in-Law

She sits cross-legged on the floor,
her corpulent figure heaped
beneath flowing robes.
Head covered by a scarf,
only her face is seen, moon-shaped.

She speaks to me, guttural, harsh sounds.
I try the little Arabic I know.
She spreads her hands and smiles,
she does not understand.
The ceiling fan whirrs gently,
but makes no inroads on
my sweat-drenched limbs.
She remains cool, serene.

I'm given hot sweet tea in a glass.
The smell of fried garlic wafts in
through the kitchen door.
Above my head hordes of flies cavort,
in the distance adhan cries.

Soon it's time to leave.
She rises and kisses me on each cheek.
Next day I return home,
Two thousand miles,
a life time away.

The Quail's Egg

The water melon seller
came every day.
He stacked the globed fruit
in a wooden cart,
small at the front,
large at the back.
He always selected
one especially for me,
then used a knife
to make a cone incision,
removing it with a flourish.

'You could do worse than marry him,'
my mother said.
But I was not untouched.
On the wedding night
my mother gave me a quail's egg
she'd filled with blood.

When the shell cracked
I wept silent tears
for the quail's lost life.

Watching the Whirling Dervish

Dazzling white swathes of cloth
swirl before my eyes, gathering
speed like an express train.
Faster and faster he dances
in fierce frenzied spin,
his body is the sun,
his breath the wind.
He defies gravity and floats free
from earthly ties.
I watch entranced,
wishing I could share
his shrouded
paradise.

Cicada Song

They moved in three years ago.
I don't know where they came from,
perhaps they fluttered in through the window
one balmy night while I slept.
At first I didn't mind the chirping,
I'd close my eyes and dream
of sipping sangrias beneath a Spanish sun.
But their Dog-Day drone went on and on.

I asked them to leave,
but they claimed squatters' rights
said they were staying
in my left ear, for the duration.
Cicada song has now become my life's refrain.
How I long for the sound
of silence once again.

Battle of the Birds

They waited in line
chirping the old familiar songs,
a real feast of a dawn chorus.
Those with the brightest
plumage puffed out their chests,
and gave the orders to fire.
Soon feathers flew,
the chirping replaced
with squawking and screeching.
One by one the birds fell.
Even the old guard toppled
off their perches.

When the slaughter had ended
an eerie silence reigned.
Shell-blasted craters were littered
with bodies, bird on bird,
eyes sparked out
beaks still standing to attention.

Verdun

Walk as far as you're allowed.
'Interdit. Verboten. Forbidden.'
For the grey earth still yields
a deadly iron harvest.

Stop and gaze around.
You'll see green undulating hills,
but they were not always there.
A hundred years ago this place was blasted
with explosives and millions of shells.
In their wake a desert terrain
of pockmarks and craters,
brimmed with soldiers' shattered remains.

Go there today and remember,
those lush mounds shroud a living hell.

Living on an Eggshell

Sometimes death rises up
from the bowels of the earth
and leaves a conversation hanging
in mid sentence,
a cake half-baked,
or a kiss clinging to the air.
It wrenches babies
from mothers' breasts,
shakes families apart
and buries them beneath
their shattered homes.
It leaves a nation writhing in despair.

A husband claws at the rubble
calling for his wife.
A father finds his child's corpse
and cries out in grief.
Bodies are piled high
in the shade of fallen trees,
their bronchial roots
withering in the midday heat.
Everywhere is the stench of death.

When the dead have been buried
the survivors will start again.
They will rebuild their homes,
brick by brick.
They will plant new crops
and dig new wells.
But they will never forget that day
the earth's crust cracked
like an eggshell.

Whale Watching

Byron Bay, our lives were looped in that place.
We spent our summers there,
riding foam-crested waves
and exploring the clear blue depths.
We snorkelled with turtles and swam
with shimmering dolphins.
Hand in hand we sauntered in the sea's lacy edge
gathering conch shells.
At night we camped beneath the stars
and talked about our dreams.
'We'll bring our children here.'

But that last time we were alone.

We drove up to 'The Cape'.
You found it hard to walk now,
so I carried you to our favourite spot.
Light as a sea sprite, your leached bones
pushed through your skin.
I brushed away sea-salt tears.
'No one lives forever,' you said.

We watched humpback whales
blow diamonds in the air
and we simply held on to each other.

Little Black Dress

It was raining when we set
off for our favourite place.
Mum was driving.
I cradled Dad in my arms.
Mum chatted about him on the way.
She told me how she used
her post office savings to buy
a little black dress for their first date
and how Gran permed her hair.
'It's important to look your best.'

When we reached the cove
the rain had stopped.
The sun scattered diamonds
on a blue-grey sea.
Mum held the urn, as we climbed the hill.
A screeching seagull wheeled
above our heads and waves
gently shifted the shingle.

'It's time to say goodbye,' Mum said.
She opened the urn and shook
the ashes over the cliff edge.
Particles like grains of sand fell
onto the grassy ledges below,
but a ghost of grey dust hung in the air.
It glittered in the sunlight
like a golden halo until snatched away
on a gust of wind.

I'll always remember that day
we said goodbye to Dad.

'Our parting date,' Mum named it.
She wanted to look her best
and so she wore her little black dress.

The Widower's House

Curtains are drawn,
doors are locked,
the loud ticking of the clock,

her perfume hangs
in the air, clings
to the cushions
on her chair.

If Dreaming is All There is

I dreamed of Dad last night
and when I woke I looked for him,
so real was my dream
it seemed he must be here.
Several minutes passed
before I knew that dreaming
was all it was.

I dreamed of Dad last night
dressed in the red cardigan I loved,
reeking of his favourite soap.
I'm sure I could smell him here.
Several minutes passed
before I knew that dreaming
was all it was.

I dreamed of Dad last night.
He kissed me in his wet-lipped way
and when I woke it felt as though
his kiss was on me still.
Several minutes passed
before I knew that dreaming
was all it was.

I hope to dream of Dad tonight
that he may speak my name
or laugh in his deep rumbling way.
And when I wake and it seems he's still here
I'll ask him why he cannot stay,
and if dreaming is all there is.

Lost in the Fog

It started as a mist:
a forgotten name,
birthday cards written –
not sent,
the telling of a recent event,
again and again.
Like a fungus it grew –
became a suffocating fog.
Now she doesn't know my face
and I can't reach her anymore,
she's lost
in some other place.

Heirloom

When I look at the clock in the hall
I'm reminded of my father:

the daily ritual winding,
precise correction of the hands

and him saying to me,
'This will be yours when I'm gone.'

Now I wind the clock
and say to my son.

'One day when I'm gone
this will be yours.'

The Race

It starts with a faltering step,
but soon they can't catch you.
You duck beneath tables,
hide behind trees.
They are breathless
and you are fearless.
Gathering speed
you come home
with grazed knees.
'Take care,' they say.
But you journey on.
You're invincible.

So you stride across foreign lands,
ski down soft snow slopes,
and bungee jump from balloons,
pausing only to dance
at friends' weddings.

Then you're dancing at your own.

Hand in hand you saunter
on sun-soaked beaches
and brush golden sand
from tiny toes.
But all too soon the sand seeps
away, others do the running now.

And you take stock.
Yes, there are regrets,
but you crack open

the champagne
and raise a glass,
'to life'.

The Man in the Moon

As a boy I laughed
at the face in the round
yellow night-light glow
that beamed through the window pane
and danced patterns on my pillow.
And I dreamed that one day we
would meet, me and the man in the moon.

When I grew up, I became part of
the race. A carefully rehearsed plan,
we were there first.
In awe I bounced around the boulders
with eyes, picked dust from the nose,
and floated over craters of teeth.
There was not one sliver of silver
or piece of green cheese in sight.

The race was won and we came home.

Now I lie here and gaze into space,
wondering how I imagined a man's face,
or reflected on rhymes about jumping cows.
Not that it really matters to me,
here in this white-walled room,
reeking of boiled cabbage and beef.

Because I, who left footprints on the moon,
am now being slowly eclipsed with all this.
Someone is holding my dish and feeding me
with a spoon.

Care Homes for Poets

They are opening care homes just for poets.
Mornings will be spent reading
and analysing favourite poems.
Life stories will be told in ballad form
and newly penned poems critiqued.
There are bound to be disagreements
over style and form with much
stamping of swollen feet.
Chair exercises will be conducted
in time with rhyme, and poetry recitals
given to family and friends.

In the afternoons the poets
will be taken into the garden
to study beads of rain on leaves,
or a hackneyed shard of sunlight
filtering through the trees.
Someone may unearth a dead fox,
cradle it in their arms and cry, 'This is my baby!'
A nurse will wrench it away saying,
'There's no more to be said.'

In the evening the poets will doze
and suck on lost-lipped mouths,
although the occasional
epitaph may be composed.
At precisely 8 p.m. the poets
will be lowered into half-baths.
Then they will be dried
and shrouded in their sheets.
Struggling to sleep they will

think of a hundred ways
to write about their dying.